I LOVE GOLF!

by Rob Stanger

Text copyright 2002 Robert Stanger
Illustrations copyright 2002 Robert Stanger

All rights reserved.

No part of this book may be reproduced in any form or by any means without permission in writing from the copyright owner. All inquiries should be addressed to: Rob Stanger at info@robstanger.com

International Standard Book Number 0-9725721-0-4

Hey you! Hey you!

Hey you!

Look over here.
In the trees, but no need to fear.

I'm **Divot**,

The
Golfing tiger
Cub.

Together
We will have
Fun,

Playing a
Game called
Golf,

Under the
Warm
Sun.

There is no game like golf,
I will prove this to you.

So come along with me,
I will show you what to do.

With **14 clubs**
You will play this game.

They fit in a **bag**
That has your name.

Golf balls and tees
Are a good source,

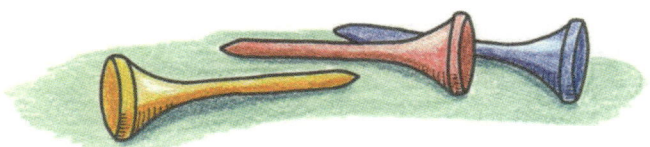

To bring with you
To the golf course.

A **golf course** has **18 holes**
That stretches out across the land.

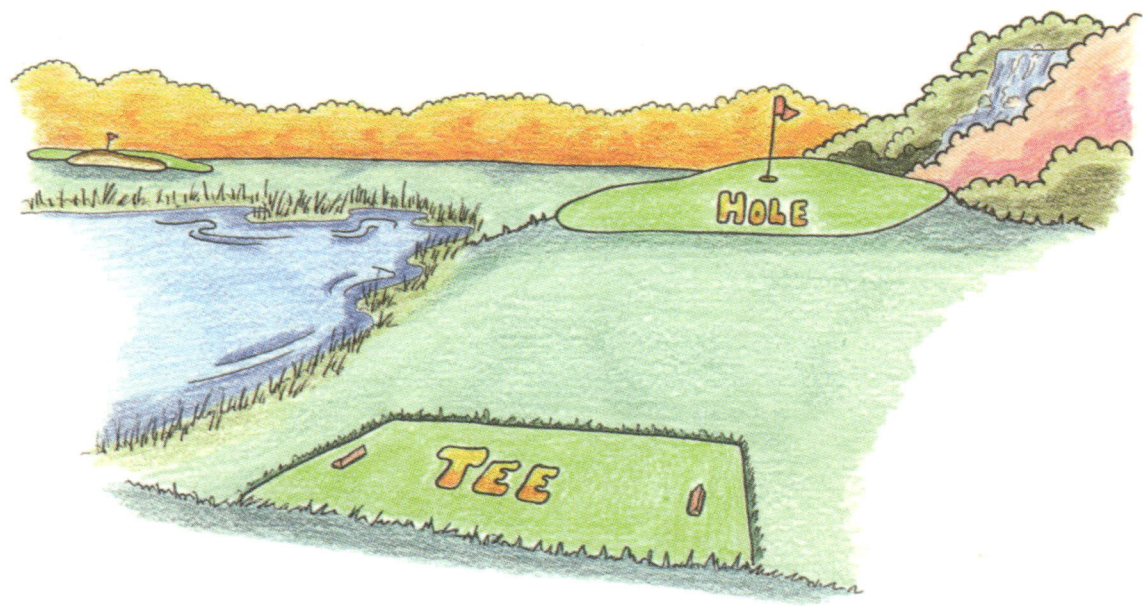

Hitting the ball into the **hole** from the **tee**,
Is your goal in the fewest **strokes** you can.

Each **hole** is given a number
To complete the task.

Par is this number,
If you were about to ask.

The length of each hole determines the par.
Par 3's for the **short holes**,

Par 4's and 5's

If they are **far!**

A **birdie**
Is one stroke **less** than par,
A **bogey**
Is one stroke **more**.

When you are playing **golf**,
This is how you keep **score**.

**But this game is not so easy,
You will soon find,
Each hole has trouble
To give you a hard time.**

I'm sorry to say so but madly it's true,
A golf course has...

Sand Traps

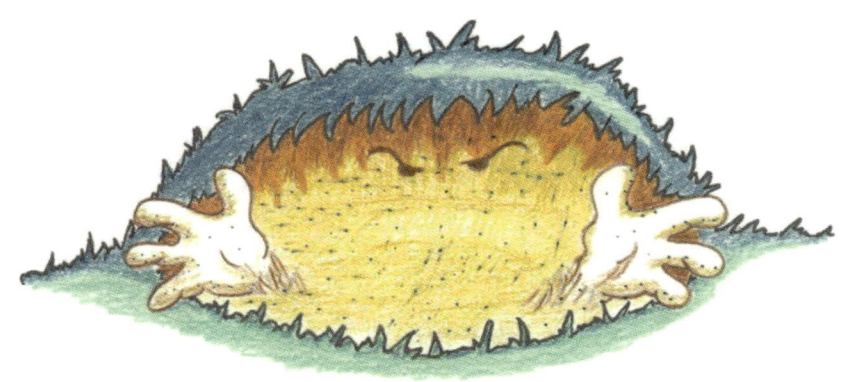

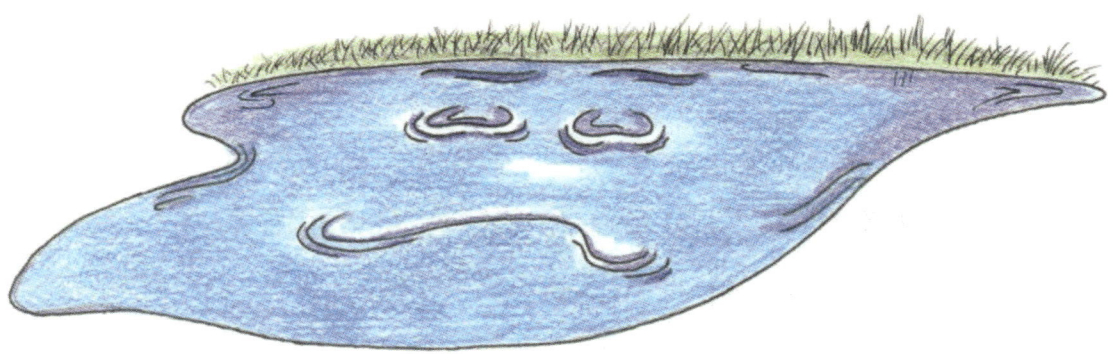

Water and

Trees

To trouble you!

So the fairways and greens
Are good places to be,
To keep your ball safe
From the trouble you see.

There is so much more for you to see,
So let's join our friends on the tee!

You will begin each hole
Hitting your ball from a tee,

Behind and **between**
The **tee markers** you see.

A good tee shot
Will help your score,

But if your ball drifts off line.....

You call out a loud FORE !

This **short grass** here
Is called the **fairway.**
To play your ball on this is the **best way.**

The **long grass** on the sides
Is called the **rough.**
Playing from there can be **tough.**

The **rough** can be **bad**,
So very **bad** you see.

Sometimes it grows so high,
You can't even see your knees.

To have the honor
Means it is your turn to play,

To that golfer who is furthest
From the hole away.

No matter where your ball lays,
Be sure to play with no delay!

The
Putting green
Is special,

A special place
On each
Hole.

Where
The grass is cut
Short...

So the ball
Can now
Roll.

Take out the **flag**,
Lay it off to the side.
Where no one is **putt**ing...

And the **ball**s can roll by.

Furthest from the hole putts **first**,
Even though their approach was the worst.

Closest to the hole putts last,
This keeps the game moving fast.

After everyone has putted out,
Write down your score with no doubt.

Back into the hole goes the flag,
And to the next tee you carry your bag.

Now that you know
The way to play this game,
The golf course is calling,
Calling YOUR name!

Come Bobby,
\ Come Vicky,
 \   Tommy and Trish.
  \ /   /
   \/   /

Come one! Come all!
This is my wish.

So grab your clubs,
A ball and a tee.

Let's go play golf!
Just You and Me.

Can you find Divot's golf words from the book?

- GOLF ✓
- CLUBS ✓
- BALL ✓
- TEE ✓
- PAR ✓
- BIRDIE ✓
- BOGEY ✓
- ROUGH ✓
- GREEN ✓
- PUTT ✓
- FORE ✓

```
G E L D I H C K L P A R U
A R B F Q F C K L B O P U
C Q E F G O L F U I U N T
C O L E G H J K L R Y U I
A M I P N H J K L D E C W
C Q D I G O L F O I G Y Q
G R S P C H C K S E O Y T
A O B F G Q R F U P B T Q
C U U F W O L F O F E E T
G O L P G H V K L P O I T
A H C F Q H N K L P O I U
C W B A L L W F O R E Y P
```

Swing into Learning
The Fundamentals of Golf !

This delightful 30 minute video demonstrates
Proper golf technique and etiquette
by Turnberry Wells, Birdie, Bogey and
Their friends in the Golf Kingdom.

Order through
www.robstanger.com
www.juniorlinks.com
www.ClubPro.com @ 1-800-467-2844